Table of Contents

Executive Summary

Almost any activity that people engage in outside the home – working, managing personal business, socializing – relies on access to transportation of some kind. And many factors, from sidewalk design to the width of the airplane aisles, affect peoples' access to transportation. Years of gathering data and conducting research have focused on identifying the transportation habits and needs of America's general population, but until now, no national data has allowed for analyses of the *specific* transportation habits and needs of people with disabilities, nor provided for contrasts to the non-disabled population. Faced with a wide spectrum of transportation demands, planners and policy makers need this kind of information in order to determine where transportation investments should be made.

The Bureau of Transportation Statistics (BTS), an operating administration within the U.S. Department of Transportation, set out to fill this data gap by developing and conducting the *2002 National Transportation Availability and Use Survey*. The survey was designed to identify the impact of transportation on the work and social lives of people with disabilities, and the extent to which such impact is unique to that population. The survey topics include:

■ the number of people with disabilities who never leave their homes because of transportation inadequacies;

■ the types of transportation people with disabilities use for local and long-distance travel;

■ their level of satisfaction with the system's ability to provide safe, accessible, reliable, efficient, affordable transportation; and

■ the barriers or challenges that are posed by the transportation environment, infrastructure, or vehicles.

All data presented in this report have been weighted to national totals. The data analysis summary compares two population groups – one comprised of people with disabilities and one comprised of non-disabled people. It also compares and contrasts challenges encountered by the two groups in their daily and non-routine travels, as well as opinions regarding their transportation experiences.

More than 5,000 people were interviewed for the survey, about half of whom had disabilities. The survey itself was developed with the participation and suggestions of various groups representing people with disabilities, and their involvement extended to every phase of the project.

The survey results indicate that:

■ More than 3.5 million people in this country never leave their homes. This is a national homebound percentage of over 1 percent. More than half of the homebound, 1.9 million, are people with disabilities. About 528,000 people with disabilities who never leave home experience transportation difficulties.

■ Regardless of disability status, personal motor vehicles are used far more frequently for local travel than any other transportation mode. The majority of people, whether with or without disabilities, drive most frequently to get to work, to doctor and medical visits, for shopping and other local travel. There is, however, a significant difference in the percentages of disabled versus nondisabled drivers. For work, about 66 percent of those with disabilities drive most frequently for local travel, compared to almost 85 percent for nondisabled drivers.

■ Proportionally, fewer people with disabilities travel long distances (100 miles or more one way) than nondisabled travelers. Among both groups, the use of personal motor vehicles (as either passenger or driver) and commercial airlines are the most frequent modes of transportation for long-distance travel.

- The *types* of difficulties encountered in using the transportation system are very similar between people with and without disabilities. Both groups report bus and airline schedules not being kept, inadequate seating on subways and airplanes, and insensitive drivers encountered while walking or biking.

Overall, the survey data indicate that much has been accomplished to provide access to transportation, and that some needed improvements cited both by people with and those without disabilities (such as the need for audible and visual signage, on-time performance) are good for everyone. The survey data indicate the need to continue to identify and correct deficiencies in hardware and schedules for public transportation, such as buses, trains, and airplanes. There is also room for progress in the softer side of travel – the "human element." Training transportation providers to be sensitive to the needs of people with disabilities and, moreover, to be prepared to provide the services to which the traveling public is rightfully entitled, is important. People with disabilities represent over 53 million citizens of all ages in this nation, and they want – and deserve – to fully participate in all this country has to offer. Further improvements in the transportation system will go far in making such participation a reality.

Freedom to Travel

Survey Goal

In terms of national transportation statistics, one area that suffers from a critical lack of information is transportation use by people with physical, mental, or emotional disabilities. Little is known about the ability of the nation's transportation system to meet the unique transportation needs of people with disabilities. The Bureau of Transportation Statistics (BTS) initiated the *2002 National Transportation Availability and Use Survey* to fill this information gap and to allow government and other researchers to analyze the data, report the results, and provide an informed basis for the development of transportation policies and programs.

The goal of this survey is to create an information resource for transportation planners and policy makers to use when developing national, state, and local policies and programs for people with disabilities.

Survey Topics

The survey gathered information in the following subject areas:

- frequency of travel outside the home, including trip purpose, mode of transportation, frequency of use of different modes, need for assistance, and satisfaction with transportation services;

- availability of paratransit (curb-to-curb service) and respondent use of paratransit;

- personal motor vehicle ownership, use, and safety issues, including vehicles modified for use by people with disabilities; and

- experiences when using various modes of travel, including difficulties with public and private transportation.

Survey respondents were asked to self-identify disability according to several definitions, specifically:

- the Census 2000 definition, which applies when one or more of the following conditions is met: **sensory** (blindness, deafness, or severe vision or hearing impairment), **physical** (substantial limitations in walking, climbing stairs, reaching, lifting, or carrying), or **long-lasting difficulties** (6 months or more) in activities affecting learning, remembering, or concentrating (**mental**); dressing, bathing, or getting around inside the home (**self-care**); going outside the home alone to shop or visit a doctor's office (**going outside the home**); and, working at a job or business (**employment**).

- the 1990 Americans with Disabilities Act (ADA) definition, which considers disability as a "physical or mental impairment that substantially limits one or more of the major life activities;" and

- if a child in the household received "special education services."

To provide comparability between the BTS survey and the decennial census, unless otherwise noted, disability data presented in this report are from respondents who self-identified their disabilities using the *Census 2000* disability definition.

Data Analysis

This section contains a summary of the disability survey data. It is divided into three sections:

- Disability Information and Travel Outside the Home
- Local and Long-Distance Personal Travel, and
- Personal Motor Vehicle Ownership and Use.

Detailed data tables showing weighted percents and standard errors for disabled and nondisabled individuals are contained in the Appendix. The purpose of this Data Analysis section is to provide *broad data findings* based on a distinction between the disabled and nondisabled groups, as classified by the Census definition. Other factors, such as the specific type of disability (e.g., vision, hearing, or physical disability), age, and severity, are not explored in this report.

DISABILITY INFORMATION AND TRAVEL OUTSIDE THE HOME

According to the 2000 decennial census, approximately 49.5 million people (19 percent) of the U.S. resident (noninstitutionalized) population aged 5 years or older have a disability (see figure 1).[1] The disability prevalence rate among children under the age of 5 years is approximately 3 percent.[2]

Frequency of Travel Outside the Home

There are 3.5 million people in this country who never leave their homes – a national homebound percentage of over one percent (see figure 2 and appendix tables 1 to 9). More than half of the homebound, 1.9 million, are people with disabilities. Overall, the majority of people with disabilities (62 percent) and those without disabilities (88 percent) leave the home five to seven days a week. People with disabilities who never leave home tend to be older (average age 66) and have more severe disabilities (58 percent report their disability as severe) than the disabled who leave home at least one day per week (average age 50, and 22 percent reporting severe disabilities). More people with disabilities who never leave home need specialized assistance

---

[1]U.S. Census Bureau, Census 2000. Summary File 3.
[2]National Center for Health Statistics. *Health United States, 2002.* Hyattsville, MD: 2002.

Figure 1
Percent of Persons Aged 5 Years or Older with Disabilities

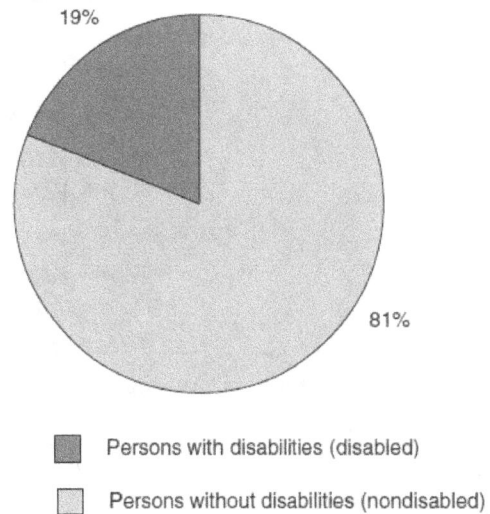

SOURCE: U.S. Census Bureau, Census 2000. Summary File

Figure 2
Number of Days Per Week People Leave Home

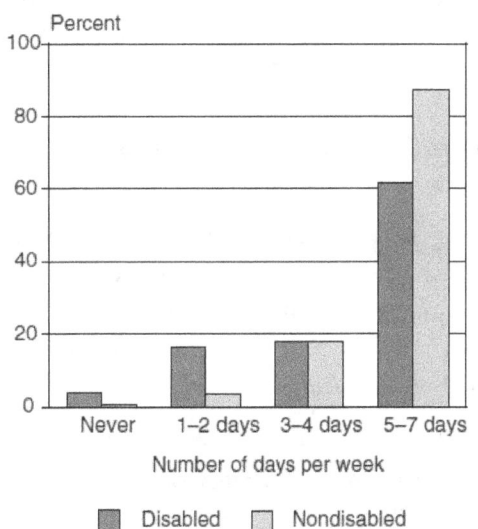

SOURCE: U.S. Department of Transportation, Bureau of Transportation Statistics, *2002 National Transportation Availability and Use Survey*

or equipment to travel outside the home (57 percent) than do those who leave home at least once a week (22 percent). And people with disabilities who never leave home also have more difficulty getting transportation (29 percent) than those who leave home once a week or more (11 percent). Of those people with disabilities who leave the home the most – five to seven days per week – 14 percent

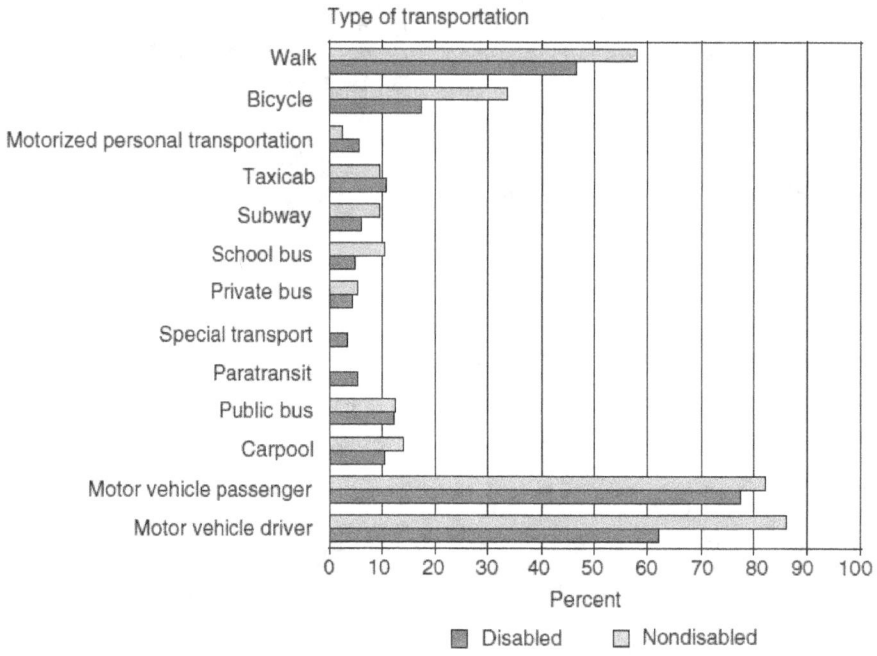

Figure 3
Transportation Modes Used in the Past Month for Local Travel

Type of transportation

SOURCE: U.S. Department of Transportation, Bureau of Transportation Statistics, *2002 National Transportation Availability and Use Survey*

need assistance to travel outside the home, and 8 percent have problems getting the transportation they need.

Specialized Assistance Traveling Outside the Home

About 23 percent of individuals with disabilities need some sort of specialized assistance or equipment to travel outside the home (see appendix tables 10 and 11). The most frequently cited types of assistance needed are:

- cane, crutches, or walker – 48 percent
- assistance from another person while outside the home – 33 percent
- manual wheelchair – 22 percent
- assistance from another person while inside the home – 16 percent
- electric scooter or wheelchair – 10 percent
- oxygen – 8 percent

Difficulties Getting Needed Transportation

Twelve percent of people with disabilities have difficulty getting the transportation they need, compared to three percent of persons without

disabilities (see appendix tables 10 and 12). The problems most frequently cited by individuals with disabilities are:

- no or limited public transportation – 33 percent
- don't have a car – 26 percent
- disability makes transportation hard to use – 17 percent
- no one to depend on – 12 percent

Of the nondisabled who have difficulty getting the transportation they need, the reason cited most often is no or limited public transportation – 47 percent.

LOCAL AND LONG-DISTANCE PERSONAL TRAVEL

Local Travel and Mode Choice

People use multiple modes of transportation for local travel. About 62 percent of people with disabilities who are 15 years or older, and about 86 percent of the nondisabled who are 15 years or older, drove motor vehicles in the month prior to the interview for local travel – to work, shopping, doctor and other medical appointments, and for other purposes (see figure 3 and appendix table 13). Seventy-seven percent of those with disabilities and 82 percent of the nondisabled rode in a personal motor vehicle as a passenger for local travel.

Forty-seven percent of people with disabilities walked (which, in this survey, includes use of a non-motorized wheelchair or scooter) for local travel during the month prior to the interview, compared to 58 percent of nondisabled persons. Similarly, a higher percentage of nondisabled respondents, 33 percent, rode bicycles or other pedal cycles compared to 18 percent of disabled persons.

A greater proportion of nondisabled persons used carpools or vanpools/group cars or vans (14 percent), school buses (11 percent), and subway/light rail/commuter trains (9 percent) than disabled persons (11 percent, 5 percent, and 6 percent, respectively) for local travel.

Of those transportation means typically provided to assist people with disabilities, only 6 percent used motorized personal transportation, such as electric wheelchairs, scooters or golf carts; 6 percent used paratransit vans or buses sponsored by the public transit authority; and 3 percent used specialized transportation services provided by human services agencies.

However, driver status appears to affect the type of transportation used in the past month (see figure 4 and appendix table 14). More than 96 percent of the disabled and nondisabled who drive, drive a personal motor vehicle for local travel. A greater proportion of the disabled and nondisabled who do not drive use carpools,; the public bus; the subway, light rail, or commuter train; and taxicabs than do the disabled and nondisabled who drive (figure 4).

Trip Purpose

Although both disabled and nondisabled workers most often use personal motor vehicles to commute to paid or volunteer work, more workers with disabilities ride as passengers (15 percent) than do nondisabled workers (6 percent), while more nondisabled individuals drive (85 percent) than do disabled individuals (66 percent) (see figure 5 and appendix tables 15 and 16).

Motor vehicles and school buses serve as the primary transportation mode for commuting to school for both the disabled and nondisabled.

Figure 4
Type of Transportation Used by Disability Status and Driver Status

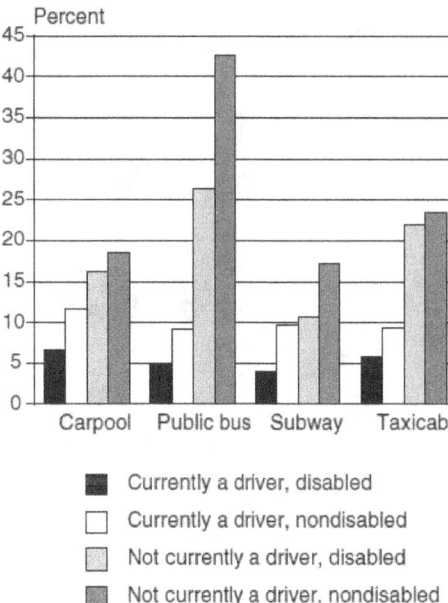

- ■ Currently a driver, disabled
- □ Currently a driver, nondisabled
- ▨ Not currently a driver, disabled
- ▨ Not currently a driver, nondisabled

SOURCE: U.S. Department of Transportation, Bureau of Transportation Statistics, *2002 National Transportation Availability and Use Survey*

About one-quarter of both disabled and nondisabled students ride a school bus, and another quarter drive a motor vehicle to school most frequently. However, 36 percent of the nondisabled students ride as a passenger in a personal motor vehicle compared to 21 percent of the students with disabilities.

Most of the disabled and nondisabled most frequently use motor vehicles, either as a driver or passenger, for transportation to the doctor and other medical visits and for other local travel, such as shopping and recreation. About 2 to 3 percent of both disabled and nondisabled use a public bus for these trips.

Transportation Availability

To some degree, transportation services are generally available to the disabled and nondisabled from their homes (see figure 6 and appendix table 17). For both groups, more than 50 percent live near a sidewalk or path, almost 60 percent have public paratransit available in the area, and over three-quarters have taxi service. About 25 percent live within 5 miles of a subway/light rail/commuter

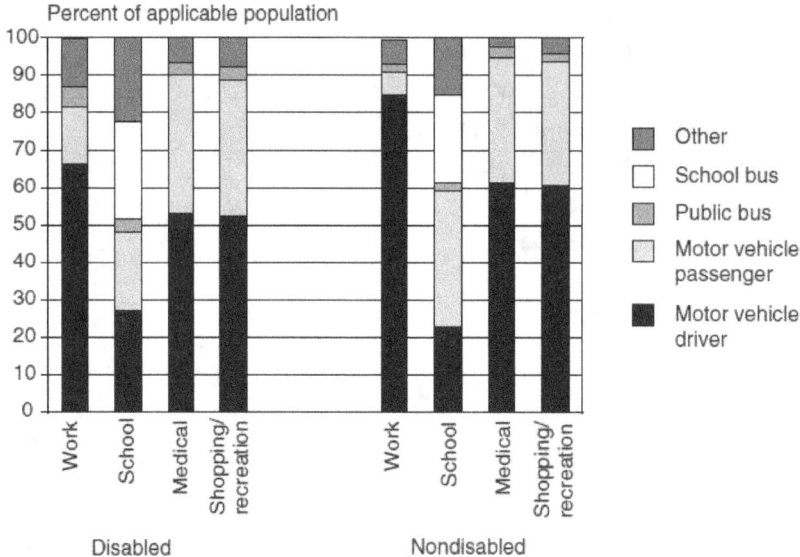

Figure 5
Trip Purpose

SOURCE: U.S. Department of Transportation, Bureau of Transportation Statistics, *2002 National Transportation Availability and Use Survey*

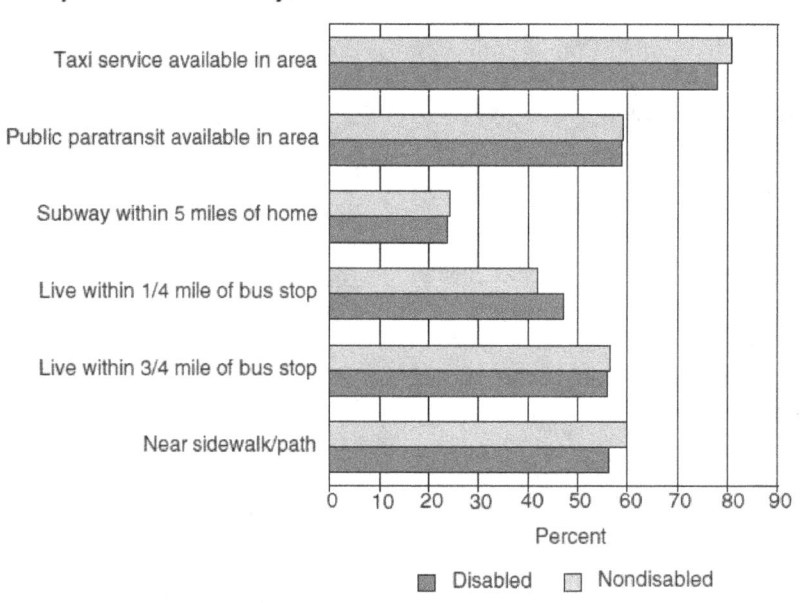

Figure 6
Transportation Availability

SOURCE: U.S. Department of Transportation, Bureau of Transportation Statistics, *2002 National Transportation Availability and Use Survey*

train station. Slightly more of the people with disabilities (47 percent) live within one-quarter mile of a bus stop than do the nondisabled (42 percent).

Transportation Use

The majority of disabled and nondisabled bus riders and subway, light rail, and commuter train users use the transportation service two or fewer days per week for local travel, as do paratransit riders[3] (see figure 7 and appendix tables 18 and 19). However, more of those with disabilities (42 percent) use the bus three or more days per week than do the nondisabled (28 percent). When using

---

[3]Paratransit is defined as service comparable to fixed-route transit for use by people with disabilities who are unable to use the fixed-route system.

Figure 7
Transit Use Frequency

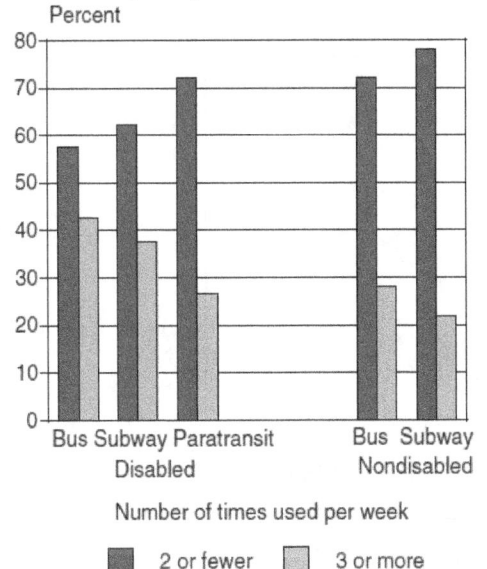

Percent

Number of times used per week

■ 2 or fewer   □ 3 or more

SOURCE: U.S. Department of Transportation, Bureau of Transportation Statistics, *2002 National Transportation Availability and Use Survey*

a bus; subway, light rail, and commuter train; or paratransit service, most riders take one or two one-way trips. More than 90 percent of disabled and nondisabled public bus users; more than 88 percent of disabled and nondisabled subway,

light rail, and commuter train users; and 95 percent of disabled paratransit users take one or two one-way trips (see appendix tables 20 and 21).

Transportation Problems

Of those who walk, bike, use paratransit, buses, or subways, fewer than half of both disabled and nondisabled transportation users experience problems as pedestrians, as cyclists, on buses, while using paratransit or at bus stops or at subway, light rail, or commuter train stations (see figure 8 and appendix tables 22 to 26). A higher percentage of disabled walkers (49 percent) experienced problems than do nondisabled walkers (37 percent).

Disabled and nondisabled transportation users cited similar problems. When walking and biking, the most frequently cited problems were insensitive drivers, too few/missing sidewalks/paths, and surface problems (potholes/cracks). The primary problem for bus and paratransit riders was schedules not being kept. On buses and on subways, light rails, and commuter trains, crowded/inadequate seating was cited by both

Figure 8
Transportation Problems

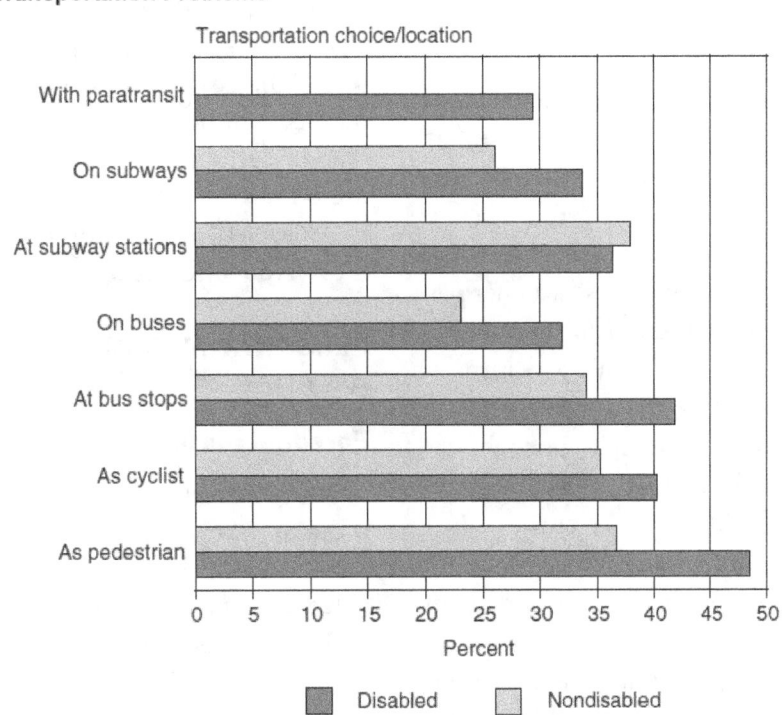

Transportation choice/location

Percent

■ Disabled   □ Nondisabled

SOURCE: U.S. Department of Transportation, Bureau of Transportation Statistics, *2002 National Transportation Availability and Use Survey*

Figure 9
Transportation Modes Used for Long-Distance Travel During Past Year

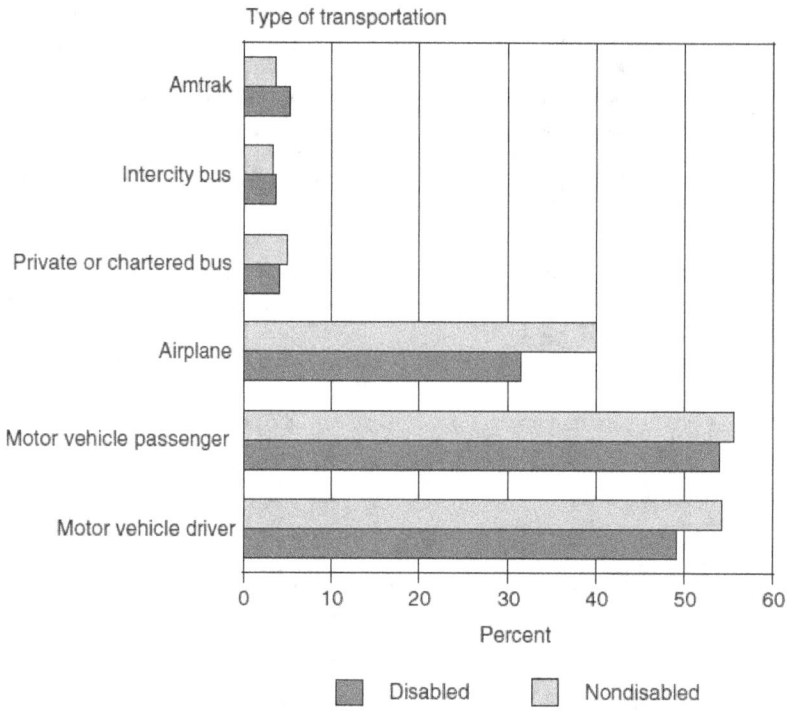

Type of transportation

SOURCE: U.S. Department of Transportation, Bureau of Transportation Statistics, *2002 National Transportation Availability and Use Survey*

disabled and nondisabled riders. Insensitive or unaware passengers were also a problem for both groups of riders.

Long-Distance Travel

Proportionally, fewer people with disabilities (60 percent) than without (76 percent) travel long distances (100 miles or more) (see appendix table 27). The two most frequently used modes of transportation for long-distance travel for both groups are personal motor vehicles (as either passenger or driver) and commercial airlines (see figure 9 and appendix table 28). Five percent or fewer of disabled and nondisabled respondents used other modes such as intercity bus (about 3 percent), private bus (almost 4 percent), and Amtrak/intercity rail (almost 4 percent).

Approximately 55 percent of air travelers with disabilities experience problems at airports compared to 45 percent of nondisabled air travelers (see appendix table 29). Although cited as problems the most frequently by both disabled and nondisabled air travelers, schedules not being

kept and restrictive security procedures were cited as problems by more of the nondisabled air travelers (38 percent and 49 percent, respectively) as compared to the disabled air travelers (25 percent and 34 percent, respectively) (see appendix table 30). Less than one-third of disabled and nondisabled persons experience problems on airplanes (see appendix table 29). Inadequate seating on airplanes was cited by more than half of the disabled and nondisabled air-travelers the most frequently (see appendix table 31).

PERSONAL MOTOR VEHICLE OWNERSHIP AND USE

Personal Motor Vehicle Usage

About 65 percent of people with disabilities drive a car or other motor vehicle compared with 88 percent of nondisabled persons. On average, disabled drivers drive 5 days per week compared with 6 days per week for nondisabled drivers (see appendix tables 32 and 33).

Thirteen percent of those with disabilities live in households that do not own or lease any

Figure 10
Percent of Drivers Who Impose Restrictions on Their Driving

	Disabled	Nondisabled
Drive less in bad weather	66.3	49.8
Drive less often than used to	64.5	32.2
Avoid driving during rush hour	58.0	42.0
Avoid busy roads and intersections	51.7	40.0
Avoid driving at night	51.5	25.8
Avoid driving distances > 100 miles	47.2	21.9
Avoid high-speed roads and highways	38.4	21.8
Avoid driving unfamiliar roads or places	38.0	27.5
Drive slower than speed limits	22.0	14.9

SOURCE: U.S. Department of Transportation, Bureau of Transportation Statistics, *2002 National Transportation Availability and Use Survey*

vehicle, 66 percent live in households that own or lease one or two vehicles, and 21 percent live in households that own or lease three or more vehicles. Among the non-disabled, only 4 percent live in households that do not own or lease any vehicles, 62 percent live in households that own or lease one or two vehicles, and 34 percent live in households that own or lease three or more vehicles. Of the 87 percent of the disabled that live in households with at least one vehicle, 2 percent own or lease a vehicle modified with adaptive devices or equipment (see appendix tables 34 to 36).

Self-Imposed Limitations to Driving

People sometimes limit their driving in different ways. More drivers with disabilities impose limitations on their driving than do nondisabled drivers (see figure 10 and appendix tables 37 and 38). Other factors, such as age, also influence the decision to impose restrictions. For example, 74 percent of the disabled drivers age 75 or older and 54 percent of the nondisabled drivers age 75 or older avoid driving at night compared to 34 percent of disabled drivers and 21 percent of nondisabled drivers, age 25 to 34.

Driving Ability Perceptions

The survey sought to determine if a person's perception of his or her driving ability as it relates to certain physical characteristics has changed from 5 years ago. Although the majority of both disabled and nondisabled drivers indicate that their capabilities are the same as they were 5 years ago, a higher proportion of disabled drivers indicate their capabilities in all categories – eyesight/night vision, attention span, hearing, coordination, reaction time to brake or swerve, and depth perception – are worse than 5 years ago (see figures 11 and 12 and appendix table 39). Of particular note, 40 percent of disabled drivers compared to 28 percent of

Figure 11
Driving Ability Perceptions by People with Disabilities

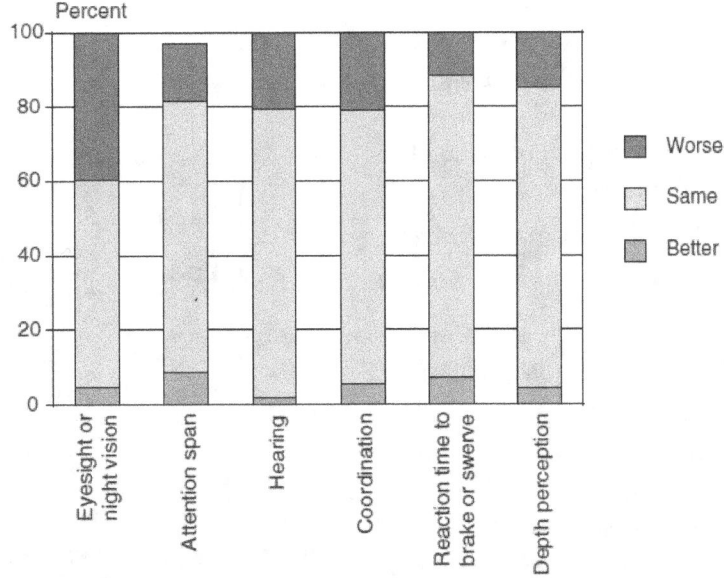

SOURCE: U.S. Department of Transportation, Bureau of Transportation Statistics, *2002 National Transportation Availability and Use Survey*

Figure 12
Driving Ability Perceptions by Non-Disabled People

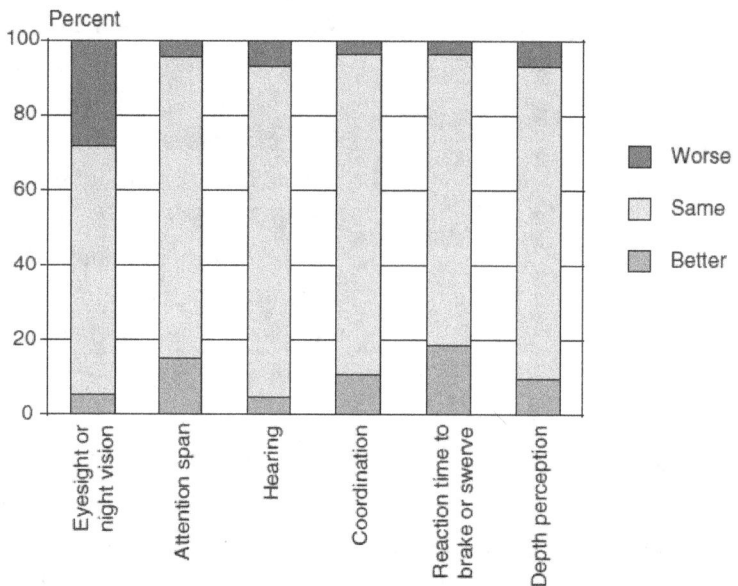

SOURCE: U.S. Department of Transportation, Bureau of Transportation Statistics, *2002 National Transportation Availability and Use Survey*

nondisabled drivers said their eyesight/night vision had declined. For the remaining categories, the percentages of drivers with a perception of declining capabilities range between 12 and 21 percent for drivers with disabilities, but only from 4 to 7 percent for nondisabled drivers. Again, these comparisons do not consider other factors such as disability type or age.

Considerations to Discontinue Driving

At some point, people may decide to give up operating a motor vehicle under certain circumstances. Approximately one-third of both disabled and nondisabled drivers indicate they would consider giving up driving if any of the following occurs:

- they feel they cannot operate a motor vehicle safely,

- their eyesight declines, or

- they experience other physical limitations.

A higher percentage of nondisabled drivers than disabled drivers indicate they would give up driving when they reach a certain age (10.2 percent of nondisabled compared to 6.4 percent of disabled) or had some other mental limitation (7.7 of nondisabled compared to 5.3 percent of disabled), while disabled drivers more often indi-

cate they would give up driving if they caused a crash (5.1 percent disabled compared to 2.9 percent non-disabled) (see figure 13 and appendix table 40). Lastly, about 10 percent of both disabled and nondisabled said they never plan to give up driving.

Figure 13
Factors Influencing Discontinuance of Driving

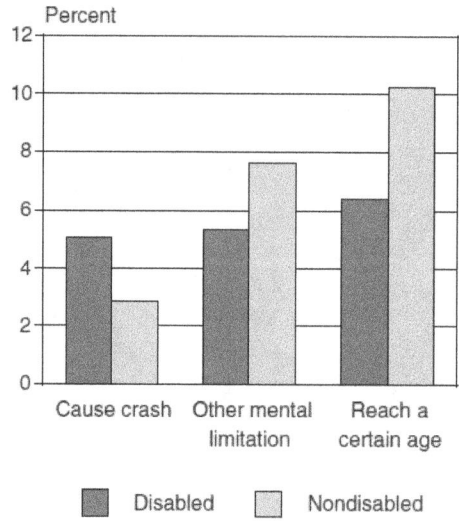

SOURCE: U.S. Department of Transportation, Bureau of Transportation Statistics, *2002 National Transportation Availability and Use Survey*

Methodology

SAMPLE DESIGN

According to the 2000 decennial census, approximately 19 percent of the U.S. resident (noninstitutionalized) population aged 5 years or older has a disability.[4]

The disability prevalence rate among children under the age of 5 years is approximately 3 percent.[5] In addition, analysis of the 1995 National Health Interview Survey on Disability (NHIS-D), using disability measures similar to those used in the decennial census, indicated that among households with disabled people, 79 percent contained only one person with a disability, 18 percent contained two disabled persons, and the remaining 3 percent contained three or more people with a disability.[6] This information was used to estimate how many *households* would need to be screened in order to interview at least 2,000 *people* with disabilities for this survey.

The sample design employed list-assisted random-digit dialing (RDD) techniques to select a nationally representative set of telephone numbers within all valid telephone exchanges in the United States. Because this was a residential survey, all business numbers were excluded. Also, because calls to cellular phones may cost the respondent at a per-minute rate, the sample frame excluded all cell numbers. However, households having only cell phones (that is, no "land line" in the household) were accounted for during the weighting process. Weighting attempts to make the estimates from a survey representative of the total population that was sampled, including making adjustments for imperfections in the sample frame.

Because of the importance of including people with disabilities in the universe from which this survey sample was selected, the sample selection process did *not* exclude any telephone numbers

---

[4]U.S. Census Bureau, Census 2000. Summary File 3. For information on confidentiality protection, sampling error, nonsampling error, and definitions, see www.census.gov/prod/cen2000/doc/sf3.pdf.

[5]National Center for Health Statistics. *Health United States, 2002.* Hyattsville, MD: 2002.

[6]1994/95 National Health Interview Survey on Disability, original tabulations from public use data files.

Table 1

Characteristics of the Civilian Noninstitutionalized Population by Age, Disability Status, and Type of Disability: 2000

	Total	
	Number	Percent
Population 5 years and over	257,167,527	100.0
With any disability	49,746,248	19.3
Population 5 to 15 years	45,133,667	100.0
With any disability	2,614,919	5.8
Sensory	442,894	1.0
Physical	455,461	1.0
Mental	2,078,502	4.6
Self-care	419,018	0.9
Population 16 to 64 years	178,687,234	100.0
With any disability	33,153,211	18.6
Sensory	4,123,902	2.3
Physical	11,150,365	6.2
Mental	6,764,439	3.8
Self-care	3,149,875	1.8
Going outside the home	11,414,508	6.4
Employment disability	21,287,570	11.9
Population 65 years and over	33,346,626	100.0
With any disability	13,978,118	41.9
Sensory	4,738,479	14.2
Physical	9,545,680	28.6
Mental	3,592,912	10.8
Self-care	3,183,840	9.5
Going outside the home	6,795,517	20.4

SOURCE: U.S. Census Bureau, Census 2000. Summary File

identified as teletype (TTY) or teledata (TDD) that would be used by people with hearing impairments.

A total of 40,000 phone numbers was released for this survey; this figure included businesses, nonworking numbers, and other cases that were ultimately purged as ineligible for the survey.

The sampling frame called for a two-staged respondent selection process. At the first stage, also called the "screener" interview phase, the household phone number was dialed and any eligible household member was asked questions pertaining to the household characteristics and whether anyone in the household had a disability. The first stage resulted in selection of a respondent for the second stage, called the "extended" interview phase. At the second stage, the selected respondent verified his disability status and then answered the remaining questions for the survey.

Of the 10,327 completed household "screener" interviews, the survey identified 2,531 households with at least one person with a disability.

SURVEY PREPARATIONS

The BTS survey design called for a household-level "screening" questionnaire (to identify whether or not a disabled person lived in the household), followed by an "extended questionnaire" for each selected person. Persons of any age (including children) were eligible to be interviewed. Proxy interviews with knowledgeable respondents were required for people under the age of 16 years, for those aged 16 to17 years who lived with adults, and for those who were unable to complete the interviews for themselves due to type or the severity of their impairments.

In order to ensure full access to the interview by all respondents, the extended (person-level) questionnaire was available by computer-assisted telephone interviewing (CATI), by mail, and by Internet. Interviewers trained in the use of teletype (TTY) or teledata (TDD) communication devices were available to interview persons with hearing difficulties.

Because, according to Census 2000, about 5 percent of residents in this country speak *only* Spanish, and again in order to promote full access to the interview for each person selected for interview, a select group of Spanish-speaking interviewers was available to administer the CATI questionnaire to respondents who spoke Spanish but not English.

Questionnaire Development

BTS provided a questionnaire draft to its contractor, Westat, a private survey research firm located in Rockville, Maryland. The contractor conducted cognitive interviews with 41 paid respondents (20 with disabilities) to ensure that the questionnaire content, flow, and response categories would yield the highest-quality survey data.

Once the CATI questionnaire was final, it was then coded for Internet response and printed for mail response in case either of these data collection modes was requested by respondents. Ultimately the internet and mail versions were also offered to mild refusals and all likely residential households where the interviewers reached answering machines. During the editing phase of the survey, the Internet and mail questionnaires were keyed into the CATI system, which resulted in a single survey database for analysis.

Interviewers

The contractor employed a total of 84 interviewers for the survey, all current or former employees with experience in telephone interviewing; there were no new hires used for this survey. All interviewers were under the direct supervision of an experienced group of supervisors, with a ratio of supervisors to interviewers of 1:5, or 20 percent.

Interviewer Training

Because only experienced interviewers were used on the project, each received 4 hours of general interviewing skills training when first hired and, in addition, had on-the-job experience with at least one CATI survey prior to the BTS survey. Every interviewer working on this survey received 16 hours of survey-specific training to become familiar with all interview-related terms, every item on the household and extended questionnaires, and all answer categories and answer-dependent skip patterns. A significant portion of the training involved sensitivity to the needs of persons with disabilities, such as interviewing those with hearing, other physical, or mental conditions.

Respondent Materials

Mailing introductory letters prior to the first telephone call to households has been shown to improve overall cooperation rates.[7] After the list-assisted RDD sample of 40,000 numbers was drawn and purged (of nonresidential or nonworking numbers), the 10,327 remaining residential cases were passed through the databases of multiple vendors to append mailing addresses for the sampled telephone numbers.

---

[7]Groves, R.M. (1989). Survey Errors and Survey Costs. New York, John Wiley and Sons.

Address matches were obtained for approximately 77 percent of all in-scope telephone numbers, and for 88 percent of all the completed interviews. Households for which mailing addresses were obtained were sent a pre-screening package containing a cover letter signed by the Director of the BTS, asking for survey cooperation, and a brochure describing the survey.

DATA COLLECTION AND RESPONSE RATES

Interviewing began on July 12, 2002 and closed out on September 29, 2002.

Computer-assisted telephone interviewing (CATI) screening was used to identify households with one or more occupants of any age with a disability. In households where only one occupant had a disability, that person was selected for the survey. In households with two or more disabled people, one person was selected using the "next birthday" method. CATI screening was also used to select respondents without disabilities from a subsample of nondisabled households, again using the "next birthday" method to identify the selected respondent. The subsampling was designed to achieve roughly equal numbers of interviews for people with disabilities and people without disabilities. This was an important component of the survey design because it provides a basis to compare the two groups and identify common transportation uses and problems as well as uses and problems unique to each group.

Each person selected in the screening phase was asked to complete a CATI "extended questionnaire" to provide detailed transportation information about his or her transportation availability, use, and satisfaction.

The target for completed "extended interviews" was 4,000 persons: 2,000 with disabilities and 2,000 without disabilities.

Respondents who initially refused participation in the survey were recontacted several times. FedEx letters, mail questionnaires, and Internet instructions were also sent to 648 households where interviewers reached an answering machine, but had not reached a household member to complete the interview.

Prior to or during interviewing, over 2,000 numbers were identified as possible fax/modem lines. Interviewers specially trained to use TTY/TDD machines called all of these numbers and, when a TTY/TDD was encountered, offered the respondent an Internet or mail verson of the survey.

Interviewers actually completed 5,019 interviews: 2,321 with disabled people (who self-identified as such through any of the disability questions asked: Census 2000, ADA, and special education) and 2,698 nondisabled people. **Please note that, although this report uses only the Census 2000 questions as the disability indicator, the public use data files and documentation include many different disability measures, allowing analysts to construct their own definition of disability using the multiple items in the survey.**

A separate variable, CDISABLD, identifies if a respondent reported one or more of the several Census disabilities. The purpose of this variable is to assist users who may want to compare the results of this survey with Census 2000 data, according to a common set of disability items. However, the decennial census collected disability information about those aged 5 years or older, while the BTS survey included persons of all ages. Therefore, when comparing the data, users should select only persons who are aged 5 years or older from the BTS dataset.

In addition to the 2000 Census disability items, this survey asked two questions about a disability related to the Americans with Disabilities Act (ADA) and one question about the receipt of special education services, which are designed for children with disabilities. A second constructed disability variable, TDISABLD, identified if a respondent reported any of the ADA items, the special education item, or the Census disability items. The purpose of this composite measure is to give the user a variable that identifies respondents reporting any of the disabilities in this survey.

The overall response rate for this survey was 56.03% and was calculated in accordance with the standards defined by the Council of American Survey Research Organizations (CASRO, 1982). This survey design required that the overall rate be computed as the product of the screener interview response rate (64.25%) and the extended interview response rate (87.21%).

DATA QUALITY

The survey implemented quality control measures at every phase. Survey methodologists reviewed the screening questions to ensure that the wording would reduce the incidence of under- or over-coverage of people with disabilities. The CATI and Internet software underwent thorough testing to ensure that the programs mimicked hardcopy questionnaire specifications. The quality control procedures during the prescreener mailing ensured that each household where an address was available was mailed a letter prior to receiving a telephone call.

Interviewers were monitored, and retrained when necessary, by management and supervisory staff from the first to the last day of data collection. Questionnaire keying (for those cases not collected by CATI) were 100% verified.

The CATI system automatically edited for correct ranges, response numbers, and inconsistencies. CATI files were repeatedly checked for consistency during the data collection period. Interviewer comments and problem sheets were reviewed daily and updated as necessary. Frequencies of responses to all data items were reviewed to ensure that appropriate skip patterns were followed.

During post-processing, BTS mathematical statisticians and data analysts carefully reviewed the data files for consistency and accuracy, and worked closely with the contractor to make any needed corrections.

WEIGHTING AND VARIANCE ESTIMATION

Weighting is a process to make the estimates from the survey representative of the total population from which the sample was drawn. It does this by accounting for the chances of selecting units into the sample and making adjustments for imperfections in the sample frame.

Survey weights were developed to reduce the bias introduced by:

- nonresponse cases,
- unknown residential status,
- nontelephone households,
- multiple telephone line households, and
- subsampling for disability status.

The weighting process began with a base weight that was adjusted to account for nonresponse and undercoverage. The base weight is the inverse of the probability of selection of the sampled unit. During the weighting process, additional information from external sources, such as the Census, was used to benchmark the weights and achieve consistency between totals from the survey data and the external sources. In order to produce estimates, weights were applied to sample data to estimate aggregate statistics. In particular, survey data were weighted to accomplish the following objectives:

- compensate for differential probabilities of selection for households and persons;
- reduce biases occurring because nonrespondents may have different characteristics from respondents;
- adjust, to the extent possible, for undercoverage in the sampling frames and in the conduct of the survey; and
- reduce the variance of the estimates by using auxiliary information.

Each final weight is the result of a series of sequential adjustments made to the base weights. As part of the weighting process, a household weight is created for all households that completed the screener interview. The household weight is the base weight computed as the inverse of the probability of selection of the sample telephone number adjusted for:

- unknown residential status,
- screener interview nonresponse,
- multiple telephone numbers,
- subsampling for disability status, and
- household poststratification.

The poststratified household-level weight is adjusted to create an individual-level (person) weight for each extended interview. The adjustments incorporate the within-household probability of selection of the sampled person and account for nonresponse. Similar to the creation of the household-level weights, each of the adjustments corresponds to a multiplicative weighting factor applied to the individual-level weight. For the individual-level weights the following factors are included:

- probability of selection of the person,
- extended interview nonresponse adjustment,
- trimming, and
- raking to person-level control totals.

A full discussion of the weighting and variance estimation procedures is available as part of the survey documentation and will be available at the BTS website when the public use data file is posted.

Data Availability

The survey public use data and documentation from BTS' 2002 National Transportation Availability and Use Survey will be posted to its Web site at: http://www.bts.gov/omnibus/targeted/index.html

As described in the "Sample Design" section of this report, the survey used a two-staged respondent selection process. The first (or "screener") stage was at the household level and the second (or "extended interview") stage was at the person level. Please note that the public use data file consists of person level records. For this reason, the counts produced from this data set are person-level rather than household-level figures. Also, because this is a person file, with only individual-level weights, many of the household-level screener variables asked at the first stage are not applicable at the person level and, therefore, do not appear in the public use data file. This includes the ADA disability questions. However, if either of the screener-level ADA items were the sole basis for identifying a person with a disability for an extended interview, this was reflected in the construction of the TDISABLD variable.

The documentation includes user notes, a codebook/data dictionary, and frequency tables for each item.

In addition to the different types of information contained in the data files, they are provided in these formats:

- SAS 8.0 format, including label statements (variable and value labels),
- SPSS 10.0 format,
- Microsoft Excel for Windows, and
- ASCII comma delimited.

BTS makes the public use data available for analytical use by anyone without prior permission from BTS, but does require that any publications using the data acknowledge the Bureau of Transportation Statistics as the data source.

Please e-mail a copy of any published analyses that use this survey's data to David Smallen, the BTS Public Information Officer, at: David.Smallen@bts.gov

BTS plans to continue to analyze the survey data and will develop Issue Briefs from the data for selected topics of interest. These can be accessed through this BTS Web site address as they become available: www.bts.gov/publications/issue_brief.

Appendix

The following tables provide documentation for the data summary section. Each table contains the weighted percent or weighted mean and the standard error. Cells with a small sample size (<30) are shaded to indicate that the weighted estimates based on a small sample size are not reliable. Cells in italics indicate a coefficient of variation greater than 30 percent and numbers are not reliable. Cells with **bold type** indicate significant differences (p <.05) between disabled and nondisabled individuals.

TABLES FOR DISABILITY INFORMATION AND TRAVEL OUTSIDE THE HOME

Table 1
Percent of Disabled and Nondisabled by Number of Days They Leave Home Per Week

	Disability status	
Days leave home per week	Disabled Percent (Standard error)	Nondisabled Percent (Standard error)
Never leaves home	3.89 (0.46)	0.72 percent (0.21)
Leaves home 1–2 days	**16.57** (1.08)	**3.53** (0.47)
Leaves home 3–4 days	**17.79** (1.25)	**7.94** (0.67)
Leaves home 5–7 days	**61.76** (1.42)	**87.61** (0.78)

SOURCE: U.S. Department of Transportation, Bureau of Transportation Statistics, *2002 National Transportation Availability and Use Survey*

Table 2
Average Age (years) of Disabled and Nondisabled by Number of Days They Leave the Home Per Week

	Disability status	
Days leave home per week	Disabled Mean (Standard error)	Nondisabled Mean (Standard error)
Never leaves home	65.65 years (3.40)	24.57 years (5.85)
Leaves home 1–2 days	**59.50** (1.50)	**27.75** (3.00)
Leaves home 3–4 days	56.65 (1.40)	29.38 (1.90)
Leaves home 5–7 days	**45.73** (0.64)	**32.35** (0.24)
Total average age	**50.73** (0.36)	**31.90** (0.13)

SOURCE: U.S. Department of Transportation, Bureau of Transportation Statistics, *2002 National Transportation Availability and Use Survey*

Table 3

Average Age (years) of Disabled and Nondisabled by Number of Days They Leave the Home Per Week

	Disability status	
Days leave home per week	**Disabled Mean (Standard error)**	**Nondisabled Mean (Standard error)**
Never leaves home	65.65 years (3.40)	24.57 years (5.85)
Leaves home at least one day a week	**50.12** (0.42)	**31.95** (0.14)
Total average age	**50.73** (0.36)	**31.90** (0.13)

SOURCE: U.S. Department of Transportation, Bureau of Transportation Statistics, *2002 National Transportation Availability and Use Survey*

Table 4

Percent of Disabled by Number of Days They Leave the Home Per Week and Disability Severity

		Disability status	
Days leave home per week	Disability severity	**Disabled Percent (Standard error)**	**Nondisabled (not applicable)**
Never leaves home	Mild	12.46 (3.61)	
	Moderate	29.53 (5.13)	
	Severe	58.01 (5.40)	
Leaves home 1–2 days per week	Mild	27.17 (4.07)	
	Moderate	39.83 (2.96)	
	Severe	33.00 (2.94)	
Leaves home 3–4 days per week	Mild	29.91 (3.47)	
	Moderate	40.41 (3.31)	
	Severe	29.69 (3.41)	
Leaves home 5–7 days per week	Mild	42.95 (2.58)	
	Moderate	40.43 (2.63)	
	Severe	16.63 (1.30)	

SOURCE: U.S. Department of Transportation, Bureau of Transportation Statistics, *2002 National Transportation Availability and Use Survey*

Table 5
Percent of Disabled by Number of Days They Leave the Home Per Week and Disability Severity

Number of days leave the home per week	Disability severity	Disabled Percent (Standard error)	Nondisabled (not applicable)
Never leaves home	Mild	12.46 (3.61)	
	Moderate	29.53 (5.13)	
	Severe	58.01 (5.40)	
Leaves home at least 1 day per week	Mild	37.84 (2.07)	
	Moderate	40.38 (1.95)	
	Severe	21.84 (1.30)	

SOURCE: U.S. Department of Transportation, Bureau of Transportation Statistics, *2002 National Transportation Availability and Use Survey*

Table 6
Percent of Disabled that Need Specialized Assistance or Equipment to Travel Outside the Home by Number of Days They Leave the Home

	Disability status	
Number of days leaves the home per week	Disabled Percent (Standard error)	Nondisabled Percent (Standard error)
Never leaves home	57.07 percent (6.38)	0
Leaves home 1–2 days per week	40.59 (4.04)	0.14 (0.16)
Leaves home 3–4 days per week	32.24 (2.94)	2.82 (1.85)
Leaves home 5–7 days per week	13.55 (1.49)	0.48 (0.20)

SOURCE: U.S. Department of Transportation, Bureau of Transportation Statistics, *2002 National Transportation Availability and Use Survey*

Table 7
Percent of Disabled that Have Difficulties Getting the Transportation Needed With Transportation by Number of Days They Leave the Home Per Week

	Disability status	
Number of days leaves the home per week	Disabled Percent (Standard error)	Nondisabled Percent (Standard error)
Never leaves home	28.79 (4.86)	0
Leaves home 1–2 days per week	19.00 (2.33)	11.71 (5.35)
Leaves home 3–4 days per week	14.17 (1.96)	2.01 (0.99)
Leaves home 5–7 days per week	8.44 (1.22)	3.15 (0.52)

SOURCE: U.S. Department of Transportation, Bureau of Transportation Statistics, *2002 National Transportation Availability and Use Survey*

Table 8
Percent of Disabled and Nondisabled by Travel Outside the Home by Need for Specialized Assistance or Equipment

	Disability status	
Number of days leave the home per week	Disabled Percent (Standard error)	Nondisabled Percent (Standard error)
Never leaves home	57.07 (6.38)	0
Leaves home at least one day per week	21.63 (1.32)	*0.66 (0.22)*

SOURCE: U.S. Department of Transportation, Bureau of Transportation Statistics, *2002 National Transportation Availability and Use Survey*

Table 9
Percent of Disabled and Nondisabled by Travel Outside the Home by Difficulties Getting Transportation Needed

	Disability status	
Number of days leave the home per week	Disabled Percent (Standard error)	Nondisabled Percent (Standard error)
Never leaves home	28.79 (4.86)	0
Leaves home at least one day per week	**11.30** (0.91)	**3.37** (0.50)

SOURCE: U.S. Department of Transportation, Bureau of Transportation Statistics, *2002 National Transportation Availability and Use Survey*

Table 10
Percent of Disabled and Nondisabled that Need Specialized Assistance or Equipment to Travel Outside the Home or Have Difficulty Getting the Transportation Needed

	Disability status	
	Disabled Percent (Standard error)	Nondisabled Percent (Standard error)
Need specialized assistance or equipment to travel outside the home	22.95 (1.26)	.66 (0.22)
Have difficulty getting the transportation needed	**12.19** (0.88)	**3.32** (0.49)

SOURCE: U.S. Department of Transportation, Bureau of Transportation Statistics, *2002 National Transportation Availability and Use Survey*

Table 11

Percent of Disabled and Nondisabled that Need Specialized Assistance or Equipment to Travel Outside the Home by Type of Assistance Needed

Specialized equipment or assistance	Disabled Percent (Standard error)	Nondisabled Percent (Standard error)
Assistance from person while inside the home	16.22 (1.87)	1.70 (1.45)
Assistance from person while outside the home	33.07 (2.95)	1.58 (1.53)
Interpreter	0.37 (0.26)	0
Professional care (rehab or counseling)	1.29 (0.52)	0
Service animal	0.21 (0.21)	0
Manual wheelchair	21.85 (2.35)	1.83 (1.49)
Electric scooter or wheelchair	10.47 (1.63)	0.83 (0.88)
Cane, crutches, or walker	48.42 (3.41)	13.87 (8.22)
Leg, arm, or back brace	4.44 (1.13)	0
Prosthetic device	1.83 (0.62)	0.40 (0.41)
Automotive adaptive aid	4.20 (0.85)	56.63 (17.69)
Public transportation aid	5.41 (1.41)	0
Hearing aid	3.28 (1.02)	0
Magnifiers or high-powered glasses	2.42 (0.86)	0
Oxygen	7.82 (1.55)	3.28 (2.09)
Medication	2.38 (0.75)	2.91 (3.12)
Other	3.00 (0.73)	1.05 (1.11)
Home modifications	1.01 (0.43)	0
Other medical equipment	6.83 (2.52)	19.36 (18.90)

NOTE: Some of the nondisabled who require specialized assistance such as motorized wheelchairs or automotive adaptive aids may not meet the Census definition of disability. For example, individuals of short stature sometimes require the use of pedal extenders to drive a motor vehicle yet are not considered to be disabled.

SOURCE: U.S. Department of Transportation, Bureau of Transportation Statistics, *2002 National Transportation Availability and Use Survey*

Table 12
Percent of Disabled and Nondisabled that Have Difficulty Getting the Transportation Needed by Type of Difficulty

Difficulty with getting needed transportation	Disabled Percent (Standard error)	Nondisabled Percent (Standard error)
Don't have a car	26.13 (3.66)	23.19 (5.56)
No or limited public transportation	33.50 (4.12)	46.62 (6.51)
No or limited taxi service	5.11 (1.52)	5.59 (2.60)
Buses don't run on time	12.88 (3.11)	13.02 (3.86)
Buses don't run when needed	8.17 (1.72)	16.86 (6.17)
Bus stops are too far away	7.64 (1.78)	10.36 (3.38)
Transportation doesn't accommodate special equipment	3.94 (1.09)	0
Disability makes transportation hard to use	16.85 (2.31)	0.38 (0.38)
Costs too much	7.35 (1.82)	3.49 (1.74)
Don't want to ask for help/inconvenience others	10.49 (2.76)	6.47 (3.40)
There's no one I can depend on	11.67 (2.35)	1.99 (1.43)
Fear of crime stops me from going places	0.93 (0.65)	4.73 (4.01)
Other	25.77 (3.42)	23.33 (6.24)

SOURCE: U.S. Department of Transportation, Bureau of Transportation Statistics, *2002 National Transportation Availability and Use Survey*

Table 13
Percent of Disabled and Nondisabled Who Used Type of Transportation in Past Month for Local Travel

	Disability status	
Type of transportation	**Disabled Percent (Standard error)**	**Nondisabled Percent (Standard error)**
Drive a personal motor vehicle such as a car, minivan, or SUV (15 years and older)	**62.40** (1.68)	**86.15** (0.83)
Ride in a personal motor vehicle as a passenger	**77.39** (1.54)	**82.07** (0.78)
Ride in a carpool or vanpool	**10.52** (1.17)	**13.92** (0.86)
Ride on a public bus such as a transit bus or city bus	12.23 (1.00)	12.59 (0.79)
Use curb-to-curb transportation provided by a public transportation authority for persons with disabilities (demand responsive service or paratransit service)	5.51 (0.52)	*1.48* *(0.49)*
Ride on a specialized transportation services provided by human service agencies	3.47 (0.46)	*2.04* *(1.43)*
Ride on private or chartered bus	4.47 (0.68)	5.52 (0.53)
Ride on a school bus	**4.91** (0.72)	**10.52** (0.71)
Ride on a subway/light rail/commuter train	**6.09** (0.75)	**9.48** (0.71)
Take a taxicab	10.75 (1.13)	9.47 (0.66)
Use an electric wheelchair, scooter, golf cart, or other motorized personal transportation	**5.59** (0.57)	**2.50** (0.38)
Ride a bicycle or other pedal cycle	**17.53** (1.33)	**33.47** (0.96)
Walk, including using a nonmotorized wheelchair or scooter, on sidewalks, at crosswalks, or intersections	**46.55** (1.75)	**57.90** (1.05)
Use another type of transportation	5.74 (0.97)	5.33 (0.49)

SOURCE: U.S. Department of Transportation, Bureau of Transportation Statistics, *2002 National Transportation Availability and Use Survey*

Table 14
Percent of Disabled and Nondisabled Who Used Type of Transportation in Past Month for Local Travel by Driver Status

Type of transportation	Currently a driver		Currently not a driver	
	Disabled Percent (Standard error)	Nondisabled Percent (Standard error)	Disabled Percent (Standard error)	Nondisabled Percent (Standard error)
Drive a personal motor vehicle such as a car, minivan, or SUV	**96.94** (0.44)	**98.55** (0.30)	N/A	N/A
Ride in a personal motor vehicle as a passenger	**71.17** (1.97)	**77.94** (0.94)	86.01 (2.53)	78.77 (3.55)
Ride in a carpool or vanpool	**6.49** (1.15)	**11.71** (0.98)	16.30 (2.64)	18.56 (3.13)
Use curb-to-curb transportation provided by a public transportation authority for persons with disabilities (demand responsive service or paratransit service)	2.02 (0.50)	*1.74* *(0.80)*	12.58 (1.61)	*2.18* *(1.61)*
Ride on a specialized transportation services provided by human services agencies	1.88 (0.54)	*3.33* *(2.53)*	6.78 (1.09)	*0.44* *(0.46)*
Ride on private or chartered bus	3.17 (0.69)	4.78 (0.60)	5.82 (1.29)	*5.41* *(1.81)*
Ride on a school bus	*2.57* *(0.89)*	5.02 (0.63)	3.43 (0.81)	10.04 (2.61)
Ride on a subway/light rail/commuter train	**4.01** (0.63)	**9.65** (0.86)	10.61 (1.96)	17.21 (3.22)
Take a taxicab	**5.82** (1.07)	**9.34** (0.71)	21.87 (2.72)	23.38 (3.46)
Use an electric wheelchair, scooter, golf cart, or other motorized personal transportation	**5.28** (0.69)	**2.88** (0.45)	6.91 (1.21)	*0.06* *(0.06)*
Ride a bicycle or other pedal cycle	**14.20** (1.76)	**25.74** (1.11)	**14.21** (2.40)	**31.11** (3.47)
Walk, including using a nonmotorized wheelchair or scooter, on sidewalks, at crosswalks, or intersections	**48.16** (2.42)	**61.54** (1.38)	**40.21** (3.11)	**52.98** (4.17)
Use another type of transportation	5.07 (0.88)	6.07 (0.60)	*6.81* *(2.49)*	*5.60* *(1.86)*

SOURCE: U.S. Department of Transportation, Bureau of Transportation Statistics, *2002 National Transportation Availability and Use Survey*

Table 15

Percent of Applicable (e.g., worker, student) Disabled and Nondisabled by Type of Transportation Used Most Often to Commute to Paid or Volunteer Work, School, Doctor or Medical Visits, and Other Local Travel, Such as Shopping and Recreation

Type of transportation	Work or volunteer		School		Doctor and medical visits		Other local travel, such as shopping and recreation	
	Disabled Percent (Standard error)	Nondisabled Percent (Standard error)	Disabled Percent (Standard error)	Nondisabled Percent (Standard error)	Disabled Percent (Standard error)	Nondisabled Percent (Standard error)	Disabled Percent (Standard error)	Nondisabled Percent (Standard error)
Personal motor vehicle as driver	**66.37** (3.02)	**84.81** (1.05)	26.99 (4.47)	22.59 (1.431)	**53.11** (1.54)	**61.07** (0.64)	**52.44** (1.66)	**60.72** (0.67)
Personal motor vehicle as passenger	**15.18** (2.53)	**5.97** (0.64)	**21.07** (3.26)	**36.45** (1.95)	36.84 (1.63)	33.65 (0.68)	**36.43** (1.54)	**32.95** (0.68)
Motorized personal transportation	0	0	0	0	0	0	0.13 (0.08)	0
Carpool or vanpool/ group car/van	1.91 (1.13)	0.42 (0.16)	3.41 (3.19)	1.17 (0.51)	0.60 (0.48)	0.04 (0.02)	0.62 (0.48)	0.10 (0.09)
Commercial airplane	0.10 (0.10)	0	0	0	0	0	0	0
Private or charter airplane	0	0	0	0	0	0	0	0
Intercity bus	0.17 (0.17)	0.03 (0.03)	0	0	0.11 (0.08)	0.02 (0.02)	0.11 (0.08)	0
Private or chartered bus	0.31 (0.20)	0.04 (0.04)	0	0.26 (0.18)	0	0	0	0
Public bus	5.34 (1.72)	2.78 (0.56)	3.68 (1.25)	2.14 (0.56)	3.36 (0.51)	2.72 (0.43)	3.35 (0.58)	2.04 (0.31)
School bus	0.18 (0.18)	0	25.76 (3.74)	23.78 (2.00)	0	0	0	0
Paratransit van/bus by public trans authority	1.45 (0.66)	0.03 (0.03)	1.68 (0.74)	0	1.23 (0.31)	0	0.57 (0.16)	0
Special transportation services by human services agency	0.56 (0.30)	0	0.65 (0.37)	0.03 (0.02)	1.09 (0.25)	0.04 (0.03)	0.24 (0.15)	0.08 (0.06)
Amtrak/intercity	0	0	0	0	0.05 (0.05)	0	0.06 (0.06)	0
Subway/light rail/or commuter train	1.40 (0.46)	1.56 (0.44)	2.85 (2.26)	0.87 (0.32)	0.55 (0.30)	0.67 (0.19)	0.49 (0.30)	0.56 (0.16)
Bicycle/pedal cycles	1.18 (0.52)	0.77 (0.23)	1.66 (0.65)	2.04 (0.57)	0.09 (0.08)	0.14 (0.08)	1.14 (0.42)	1.36 (0.26)
Taxicab	0.65 (0.28)	0.09 (0.05)	0	0	1.25 (0.31)	0.27 (0.10)	1.09 (0.32)	0.36 (0.15)
Works at home/home-schooled	0.92 (0.32)	0.94 (0.33)	2.09 (1.38)	0.46 (0.28)	0	0	0	0
Telecommutes	0	0	0.85 (0.71)	0.078 (0.08)	0	0	0	0
Walking/nonmotorized wheelchair	2.93 (0.88)	2.21 (0.47)	5.98 (2.77)	9.20 (1.34)	1.37 (0.50)	1.27 (0.29)	2.77 (0.73)	1.61 (0.35)
Other transportation	1.37 (0.50)	0.36 (0.13)	3.35 (1.13)	0.95 (0.43)	0.35 (0.16)	0.11 (0.09)	0.56 (0.17)	0.24 (0.11)

SOURCE: U.S. Department of Transportation, Bureau of Transportation Statistics, *2002 National Transportation Availability and Use Survey*

Table 16

Percent of Applicable (e.g., worker, student) Disabled and Nondisabled by Type of Transportation Used Most Often to Commute toPaid or Volunteer Work, School, Doctor or Medical Visits, and Other Local Travel, Such as Shopping and Recreation

Type of transportation	Work or volunteer		School		Doctor and medical visits		Other local travel, such as shopping and recreation	
	Disabled Percent (Standard error)	Nondisabled Percent (Standard error)	Disabled Percent (Standard error)	Nondisabled Percent (Standard error)	Disabled Percent (Standard error)	Nondisabled Percent (Standard error)	Disabled Percent (Standard error)	Nondisabled Percent (Standard error)
Personal motor vehicle as driver	**66.37** (3.02)	**84.81** (1.05)	26.99 (4.47)	22.59 (1.43)	**53.11** (1.54)	**61.07** (0.64)	**52.44** (1.66)	**60.72** (0.67)
Personal motor vehicle as passenger	**15.18** (2.53)	**5.97** (0.64)	21.07 (3.26)	36.45 (1.95)	36.84 (1.63)	33.65 (0.68)	**36.43** (1.54)	**32.93** (0.68)
Public bus	*5.34* *(1.72)*	2.78 (0.56)	*3.68* *(1.25)*	2.14 (0.56)	3.36 (0.51)	2.72 (0.43)	3.35 (0.58)	2.04 (0.31)
School bus	*0.18* *(0.18)*	0	25.76 (3.74)	23.78 (2.00)	0	0	0	0
Other transportation	**12.94** (1.84)	**6.44** (0.73)	22.51 (4.46)	15.05 (1.54)	**6.68** (0.84)	**2.55** (0.41)	**7.79** (0.97)	**4.31** (0.49)

SOURCE: U.S. Department of Transportation, Bureau of Transportation Statistics, *2002 National Transportation Availability and Use Survey*

Table 17

Percent of Disabled and Nondisabled by Availability of Transportation

Availability	Disability status	
	Disabled Percent (Standard error)	Nondisabled Percent (Standard error)
Near sidewalk/path	56.27 (1.56)	59.87 (1.17)
Live within ¾ mile of bus stop	55.86 (1.39)	56.60 (1.13)
Live within ¼ mile of bus stop	**46.55** (1.53)	**42.42** (1.08)
Subway/light rail/commuter train within 5 miles of home	23.53 (1.38)	24.06 (0.88)
Public paratransit available in area	58.25 (1.86)	59.16 (1.36)
Taxi service available in area	77.97 (1.44)	80.77 (0.95)

SOURCE: U.S. Department of Transportation, Bureau of Transportation Statistics, *2002 National Transportation Availability and Use Survey*

Table 18

Percent of Disabled and Nondisabled Transportation Users by Number of Days Per Week Use Transportation in the Past Month

Number of days per week	Public bus		Subway, light rail, or commuter train		Public paratransit	
	Disabled Percent (Standard error)	Nondisabled Percent (Standard error)	Disabled Percent (Standard error)	Nondisabled Percent (Standard error)	Disabled Percent (Standard error)	Nondisabled Percent (Standard error)
<1	24.01 (3.63)	29.72 (3.43)	34.19 (6.51)	37.29 (3.66)	38.07 (5.49)	49.30 (17.20)
1	**16.75** (3.05)	**27.43** (2.96)	18.86 (4.19)	26.72 (3.21)	21.69 (4.81)	8.90 (7.95)
2	16.75 (4.10)	14.92 (2.62)	9.19 (2.87)	14.07 (2.99)	13.45 (3.98)	0
3	15.62 (3.33)	8.18 (1.76)	15.72 (7.32)	3.83 (1.32)	14.58 (3.23)	7.94 (8.52)
4	3.87 (1.36)	6.75 (1.98)	6.67 (4.50)	1.72 (0.81)	4.38 (2.77)	16.75 (12.63)
5	16.75 (5.38)	9.43 (2.12)	11.26 (3.49)	14.01 (2.82)	7.82 (2.23)	17.10 (10.09)
6	2.66 (1.12)	2.76 (1.37)	0.43 (0.44)	0	0	0
7	3.77 (1.52)	0.80 (0.28)	3.68 (2.20)	2.35 (1.33)	0	0
Mean days	**2.50** (0.20)	**1.93** (0.13)	2.13 (0.21)	1.78 (0.17)	1.68 (0.16)	2.10 (0.61)

SOURCE: U.S. Department of Transportation, Bureau of Transportation Statistics, *2002 National Transportation Availability and Use Survey*

Table 19

Percent of Disabled and Nondisabled Transportation Users by Number of Days Per Week Use Transportation in the Past Month

Number of days per week	Public bus		Subway, light rail, or commuter train		Public paratransit	
	Disabled Percent (Standard error)	Nondisabled Percent (Standard error)	Disabled Percent (Standard error)	Nondisabled Percent (Standard error)	Disabled Percent (Standard error)	Nondisabled Percent (Standard error)
2 or fewer	**57.50** (5.14)	**72.07** (3.23)	62.24 (7.49)	78.09 (3.51)	73.21 (4.47)	58.21 (16.36)
3 or more	**42.50** (5.14)	**27.93** (3.23)	37.76 (7.49)	21.91 (3.51)	26.79 (4.47)	41.79 (16.36)

SOURCE: U.S. Department of Transportation, Bureau of Transportation Statistics, *2002 National Transportation Availability and Use Survey*

Table 20

Percent of Disabled and Nondisabled Transportation Users by Number of One-Way Trips a Day

	Public bus		Subway, light rail, or commuter train		Public paratransit	
Number of one-way trips a day	Disabled Percent (Standard error)	Nondisabled Percent (Standard error)	Disabled Percent (Standard error)	Nondisabled Percent (Standard error)	Disabled Percent (Standard error)	Nondisabled Percent (Standard error)
1	33.19 (5.07)	34.39 (3.26)	25.85 (6.02)	29.43 (3.84)	40.56 (6.20)	56.98 (17.02)
2	60.27 (4.90)	57.30 (3.57)	62.14 (6.59)	62.48 (4.22)	55.15 (6.12)	43.02 (17.02)
3	3.80 (1.40)	2.78 (1.00)	8.33 (5.41)	3.17 (1.42)	0.88 (0.88)	0
4	1.77 (0.77)	4.01 (1.64)	1.43 (1.08)	2.89 (1.17)	2.34 (1.48)	0
5	0.44 (0.44)	0.69 (0.68)	1.83 (1.87)	1.18 (1.20)	0	0
6	0.55 (0.42)	0.20 (0.14)	0.42 (0.42)	0.57 (0.40)	0	0
7	0	0	0	0	0	0
8	0	0.09 (0.09)	0	0	0	0
9	0	0	0	0	0	0
10	0	0.53 (0.53)	0	0.28 (0.28)	1.08 (1.09)	0

SOURCE: U.S. Department of Transportation, Bureau of Transportation Statistics, *2002 National Transportation Availability and Use Survey*

Table 21

Percent of Disabled and Nondisabled Transportation Users by Number of One-Way Trips a Day

	Public bus		Subway, light rail, or commuter train		Public paratransit	
Number of one-way trips a day	Disabled Percent (Standard error)	Nondisabled Percent (Standard error)	Disabled Percent (Standard error)	Nondisabled Percent (Standard error)	Disabled Percent (Standard error)	Nondisabled Percent (Standard error)
1–2	93.45 (1.68)	91.69 (2.11)	87.99 (5.60)	91.91 (2.64)	95.71 (2.02)	100.00 0
More than 2	6.55 (1.68)	8.31 (2.11)	12.01 (5.60)	8.09 (2.64)	4.29 (2.02)	0

SOURCE: U.S. Department of Transportation, Bureau of Transportation Statistics, *2002 National Transportation Availability and Use Survey*

Table 22
Percent of Disabled and Nondisabled Experiencing Problems with Local Transportation

	Disability status	
Type of transportation	Disabled Percent (Standard error)	Nondisabled Percent (Standard error)
As a pedestrian	**48.60** (2.57)	**36.75** (1.35)
As a cyclist	40.15 (4.57)	35.23 (1.87)
At bus stops	41.77 (4.96)	33.99 (3.43)
On a the bus	31.91 (4.29)	23.15 (2.77)
At subway/light rail/commuter train stations	36.46 (6.59)	38.02 (3.95)
While on the subway/light rail/commuter trains	33.64 (5.51)	26.00 (3.52)
Public paratransit service	29.42 (5.98)	34.09 (17.98)

SOURCE: U.S. Department of Transportation, Bureau of Transportation Statistics, *2002 National Transportation Availability and Use Survey*

Table 23
Percent of Disabled and Nondisabled Experiencing Problems as a Pedestrian or as a Cyclist for Local Travel

	As a pedestrian		As a cyclist	
Problems	Disabled Percent (Standard error)	Nondisabled Percent (Standard error)	Disabled Percent (Standard error)	Nondisabled Percent (Standard error)
Audible/visual/tactile info limited	3.71 (1.92)	2.49 (0.75)	1.59 (0.82)	0.98 (0.28)
Crosswalk time too short	11.31 (2.94)	6.37 (1.05)	1.16 (0.86)	1.10 (0.61)
Crosswalks not marked/missing	11.22 (2.50)	11.88 (1.70)	7.32 (6.27)	5.53 (1.55)
Curb cut/ramp/stair/grade problems	7.48 (1.05)	5.55 (1.16)	7.42 (5.79)	3.01 (1.43)
Difficult to see/be seen	3.08 (1.02)	1.47 (0.49)	3.55 (2.01)	3.97 (1.30)
Don't know when it's safe to cross	10.94 (2.46)	7.14 (1.48)	3.15 (1.96)	2.89 (1.42)
Drainage poor	3.11 (2.30)	0.14 (0.14)	0	0.89 (0.64)
Drivers don't stop for me	16.44 (2.39)	18.55 (1.83)	11.93 (4.10)	12.16 (1.77)
Grates and gaps	1.08 (0.48)	1.80 (0.66)	0.38 (0.39)	1.29 (0.74)
Insensitive/unaware drivers	24.34 (2.85)	25.09 (2.32)	26.87 (6.93)	24.36 (2.62)
Insensitive/unaware pedestrians	1.86 (0.72)	4.12 (1.06)	1.81 (1.35)	3.56 (1.25)
Lighting inadequate	3.76 (2.29)	1.74 (0.70)	1.44 (1.17)	0.67 (0.51)

(continued)

Table 23
Percent of Disabled and Nondisabled Experiencing Problems as a Pedestrian or as a Cyclist for Local Travel (Continued)

Problems	As a pedestrian		As a cyclist	
	Disabled Percent (Standard error)	Nondisabled Percent (Standard error)	Disabled Percent (Standard error)	Nondisabled Percent (Standard error)
Median/island problems	0.91 (0.50)	0.61 (0.31)	1.15 (0.83)	0
Moving traffic too close to me	3.73 (1.02)	5.40 (1.02)	16.74 (6.08)	15.07 (1.83)
Obstacles/protusions/low clearance	5.50 (1.09)	5.65 (1.27)	5.11 (3.21)	5.47 (1.29)
Passing space/width limited	3.13 (0.76)	1.81 (0.59)	13.14 (6.02)	10.08 (1.88)
Surface problems (potholes/cracks)	21.43 (2.66)	22.05 (1.91)	18.07 (5.52)	12.30 (1.96)
Too few/missing sidewalks/paths	**19.05** (2.99)	**29.90** (2.30)	29.81 (4.92)	40.41 (3.34)
Other problems	4.93 (2.28)	1.59 (0.64)	7.24 (3.36)	2.78 (1.11)

SOURCE: U.S. Department of Transportation, Bureau of Transportation Statistics, *2002 National Transportation Availability and Use Survey*

Table 24
Percent of Disabled and Nondisabled Experiencing Problems at Bus Stops or at Subway/Light Rail/Commuter Train Stations for Local Travel

Problems	At bus stops		At subway/light rail/commuter train stations	
	Disabled Percent (Standard error)	Nondisabled Percent (Standard error)	Disabled Percent (Standard error)	Nondisabled Percent (Standard error)
Audible/visual/tactile info limited	1.37 (1.00)	2.66 (1.43)	9.23 (4.55)	11.13 (3.49)
Crowding/seating inadequate	16.43 (4.01)	9.08 (2.61)	15.92 (6.37)	19.02 (5.07)
Curb cut/ramp/stair/grade problems	2.54 (1.47)	0	2.89 (2.24)	1.29 (0.91)
Difficult to see/be seen	0	0	0	0
Drainage poor	0	0	0	0
Elevators/escalators broken/missing	0	0	11.49 (5.45)	5.73 (2.34)
Fare difficult to purchase	0	1.65 (1.67)	5.65 (3.51)	8.32 (2.99)
Insensitive/unaware passengers	11.59 (3.37)	2.39 (1.58)	0	2.02 (1.30)
Lighting inadequate	2.68 (1.68)	4.09 (2.40)	2.85 (2.08)	0
Obstacles/protusions/debris	2.49 (1.32)	9.22 (3.87)	1.11 (1.11)	4.10 (3.02)
Passenger travel info inadequate	0.59 (0.60)	6.63 (3.13)	7.80 (4.70)	2.80 (1.87)
Passing space/aisle width limited	0.50 (0.48)	0	1.12 (1.10)	0
Personal safety concerns	15.55 (3.94)	2.89 (1.67)	10.80 (4.89)	9.40 (2.83)

(continued)

Table 24

Percent of Disabled and Nondisabled Experiencing Problems at Bus Stops or at Subway/Light Rail/Commuter Train Stations for Local Travel (Continued)

Problems	At bus stops		At subway/light rail/commuter train stations	
	Disabled Percent (Standard error)	Nondisabled Percent (Standard error)	Disabled Percent (Standard error)	Nondisabled Percent (Standard error)
Restroom facilities inadequate	0	3.56 (2.48)	7.49 (5.68)	1.91 (1.81)
Schedule not kept	41.64 (6.80)	49.30 (5.54)	21.10 (14.27)	26.04 (6.55)
Shelter inadequate	20.18 (5.50)	29.94 (5.91)	3.10 (2.98)	4.88 (2.41)
Staff assistance/sensitivity poor	8.20 (3.25)	5.39 (3.25)	3.36 (2.61)	2.77 (2.01)
Surface problem (potholes/cracks)	0.90 (0.87)	1.99 (1.81)	0	0
To few/missing sidewalks/paths	3.01 (1.52)	3.64 (3.04)	0	0
Vehicle does not always stop for me	6.39 (3.23)	11.54 (4.90)	Not applicable	Not applicable
Wide gaps between platforms and cars	Not applicable	Not applicable	0	0
Parking inadequate	0	1.02 (0.72)	2.04 (2.11)	6.34 (3.01)
Other bus or train problem	11.37 (5.84)	4.39 (3.59)	15.18 (6.44)	10.56 (3.14)
Personal comfort	Not applicable	Not applicable	14.51 (10.37)	12.16 (4.04)
Service not available	12.40 (3.93)	9.28 (3.71)	Not applicable	Not applicable

SOURCE: U.S. Department of Transportation, Bureau of Transportation Statistics, *2002 National Transportation Availability and Use Survey*

Table 25

Percent of Disabled and Nondisabled Experiencing Problems on Buses or on Subway/Light Rail/Commuter Trains for Local Travel

Problems	On buses		On subway/light rail/commuter trains	
	Disabled Percent (Standard error)	Nondisabled Percent (Standard error)	Disabled Percent (Standard error)	Nondisabled Percent (Standard error)
Audible/visual/tactile info limited	3.04 (2.16)	1.25 (1.18)	6.31 (4.31)	11.88 (4.43)
Board/exit time inadequate	3.37 (1.85)	5.58 (4.38)	6.42 (3.79)	3.53 (2.56)
Boarding/exiting equipment limited	4.08 (2.78)	1.66 (1.55)	5.51 (5.02)	5.04 (4.03)
Crowding/seating inadequate	45.87 (7.71)	27.86 (5.46)	26.64 (8.35)	38.96 (7.59)
Difficult to board/exit	5.61 (2.62)	0.81 (0.83)	7.57 (4.08)	1.96 (1.67)
Equipment storage inadequate	1.12 (0.83)	0	0	0
Fare purchase difficult	0.77 (0.77)	0.84 (0.87)	0	0

(continued)

Table 25

Percent of Disabled and Nondisabled Experiencing Problems on Buses or on Subway/Light Rail/Commuter Trains for Local Travel (Continued)

Problems	On buses		On subway/light rail/commuter trains	
	Disabled Percent (Standard error)	Nondisabled Percent (Standard error)	Disabled Percent (Standard error)	Nondisabled Percent (Standard error)
Insensitive/unaware driver	16.42 (4.80)	12.51 (5.94)	3.36 (3.18)	1.10 (1.09)
Insensitive/unaware passengers	31.30 (6.48)	32.16 (6.92)	15.74 (6.21)	21.32 (5.49)
Lighting inadequate	0	0	10.95 (9.93)	0
Obstacles/protusions	4.20 (2.15)	2.86 (2.01)	1.65 (1.72)	5.17 (2.37)
Passenger travel info inadequate	0	2.53 (2.57)	0	2.37 (1.60)
Passing space/aisle width limited	4.66 (2.61)	0	5.51 (5.02)	0
Personal safety concerns	13.3 (4.77)	10.76 (6.12)	15.22 (6.53)	16.28 (4.51)
Restroom facilities inadequate	0	0.81 (0.83)	5.51 (5.02)	0.77 (0.77)
Service animals not permitted	0	0	0	0
Staff assistance/sensitivity poor	4.69 (2.77)	12.15 (5.60)	3.36 (3.18)	0
Wheelchair space inadequate	0	0	0	0
Other bus or train problem	11.52 (4.56)	6.96 (3.09)	8.84 (4.63)	10.84 (4.07)
Personal comfort	3.89 (2.00)	13.33 (4.77)	24.55 (11.31)	11.38 (4.50)

SOURCE: U.S. Department of Transportation, Bureau of Transportation Statistics, *2002 National Transportation Availability and Use Survey*

Table 26
Percent of Disabled Experiencing Problems on Paratransit for Local Travel

Problems	Disabled Percent (Standard error)	Nondisabled Percent (Standard error)
Attendant/escort service limited	1.90 (1.78)	0
Cannot schedule repeating trips	3.37 (3.48)	0
Cost is too high	0	0
Difficult to board/exit	4.15 (2.73)	0
Inadequate seating	0	0
Insensitive/unaware driver	13.19 (8.62)	0
Personal safety concerns	12.91 (8.08)	0
Responsiveness problems	5.82 (4.00)	11.07 (12.35)
Schedule for pickup not kept/long waits	52.56 (9.90)	88.93 (12.35)
Schedule for drop-off not kept/long wait	40.85 (8.94)	0
Service often not available when need it	5.55 (3.11)	0
Staff assistance/sensitivity inadequate	0	0
Vehicle is in poor mechanical condition	10.13 (7.84)	0
Vehicle not accessible	3.95 (2.82)	0
Trip time is too variable/unpredictable	17.80 (8.52)	0
Other paratransit problem	23.08 (10.35)	0

SOURCE: U.S. Department of Transportation, Bureau of Transportation Statistics, *2002 National Transportation Availability and Use Survey*

Table 27
Percent of Disabled and Nondisabled who Made Long-Distance Trips of 100 Miles or More One-Way Last Year

Long distance travel	Disability status	
	Disabled Percent (Standard error)	Nondisabled Percent (Standard error)
Traveled long distance in last year	**59.95** (1.55)	**76.32** (0.99)

SOURCE: U.S. Department of Transportation, Bureau of Transportation Statistics, *2002 National Transportation Availability and Use Survey*

Table 28

Percent of Disabled and Nondisabled by Type of Transportation Used for Long-Distance Travel in Past Year

Types of transportation	Disability status	
	Disabled **Percent** **(Standard error)**	**Nondisabled** **Percent** **(Standard error)**
Private motor vehicle as a driver	**49.22** (2.27)	**54.27** (1.11)
Private motor vehicle as a passenger	53.94 (2.17)	55.57 (1.18)
Motorized personal transportation	0.20 (0.12)	0.11 (0.09)
Carpool or vanpool/group car or van	0.78 (0.28)	1.32 (0.29)
Commercial airline	**31.49** (2.01)	**40.10** (1.25)
Private or charter airplane	1.40 (0.84)	1.31 (0.26)
Intercity bus	3.49 (0.93)	3.21 (0.45)
Private or chartered bus	4.02 (0.57)	4.85 (0.58)
Public bus	1.63 (0.45)	1.10 (0.30)
School bus	0.59 (0.21)	1.18 (0.28)
Paratransit van/bus by public transit authority	0.20 (0.14)	0.10 (0.08)
Special transport served by human service agency	0.26 (0.12)	0
Amtrak/intercity	5.15 (1.12)	3.59 (0.42)
Subway/light rail/commuter train	1.59 (0.63)	2.37 (0.37)
Bicycle/pedal cycles	0.21 (0.03)	0.57 (0.17)
Taxicab	0.83 (0.28)	1.26 (0.24)
Works at home/home-schooled	0	0.05 (0.05)
Telecommutes	0.18 (0.13)	0.06 (0.05)
Walking	0.31 (0.12)	0.70 (0.23)
Other transportation	5.78 (1.18)	4.00 (0.52)

SOURCE: U.S. Department of Transportation, Bureau of Transportation Statistics, *2002 National Transportation Availability and Use Survey*

Table 29
Percent of Disabled and Nondisabled Experiencing Problems with Long-Distance Travel

	Disability status	
Type of transportation	Disabled Percent (Standard error)	Nondisabled Percent (Standard error)
At airports	**54.50** (4.19)	**44.94** (1.92)
On airplanes	32.91 (4.47)	23.61 (1.77)
At intercity bus stations	62.41 (18.26)	17.52 (6.19)
On intercity buses	54.45 (20.84)	22.85 (7.18)
At train stations	23.48 (7.35)	32.63 (5.86)
On trains	12.83 (4.74)	30.64 (5.87)

SOURCE: U.S. Department of Transportation, Bureau of Transportation Statistics, *2002 National Transportation Availability and Use Survey*

Table 30
Percent of Disabled and Nondisabled Experiencing Problems at Airports During Long-Distance Travel

Problems	Disabled Percent (Standard error)	Nondisabled Percent (Standard error)
Audible/visual/tactile info limited	2.30 (0.91)	0.79 (0.42)
Curb cut/ramp/stair/grade problems	0.65 (0.48)	0.25 (0.17)
Difficult to see/be seen	0	0
Drainage poor	0	0
Elevators/escalators broken/missing	0.65 (0.48)	0.08 (0.08)
Fare purchase difficult	1.57 (0.91)	1.04 (0.67)
Insensitive/unaware passengers	0.56 (0.32)	2.15 (0.92)
Lighting inadequate	0.41 (0.42)	0.47 (0.47)
Obstacles/protusions/debris	0.83 (0.50)	1.46 (0.69)
Passenger travel info inadequate	3.81 (1.57)	2.94 (1.03)
Passing space/aisle width limited	2.17 (1.27)	1.26 (0.55)
Personal assistant not allowed	0.35 (0.21)	0.31 (0.20)
Personal safety concerns	3.08 (1.08)	3.29 (1.10)
Restroom facilities inadequate	0	1.46 (0.64)

(continued)

Table 30
Percent of Disabled and Nondisabled Experiencing Problems at Airports During Long-Distance Travel (Continued)

Problems	Disabled Percent (Standard error)	Nondisabled Percent (Standard error)
Schedule not kept	**25.39** (4.07)	**37.66** (3.50)
Seating inadequate	9.80 (4.62)	5.93 (1.80)
Security procedures too restrictive	**34.12** (4.28)	**49.18** (3.45)
Shelter inadequate	0	0.23 (0.23)
Staff assistance/sensitivity poor	15.92 (4.50)	5.86 (1.17)
Surface problems(potholes/cracks)	0	0
Ticket counters too high	0	0.48 (0.45)
Too few/missing sidewalks/paths	0	0
Tram/moving sidewalk problem	1.73 (0.78)	0.74 (0.30)
Unable to communicate with staff	0.55 (0.34)	0.94 (0.64)
Wheelchair unavailable	4.95 (2.29)	0
Parking inadequate	3.71 (1.25)	2.88 (0.95)
Other airline problem	15.41 (4.15)	10.44 (1.86)
Too much walking required	8.84 (2.11)	0.89 (0.57)
Lost/mistreated luggage	2.85 (1.12)	2.10 (0.69)
Security inadequate/insufficient	1.74 (0.83)	3.07 (0.91)

SOURCE: U.S. Department of Transportation, Bureau of Transportation Statistics, *2002 National Transportation Availability and Use Survey*

Table 31
Percent of Disabled and Nondisabled Experiencing Problems on Airplanes During Long-Distance Travel

Problems	Disabled Percent (Standard error)	Nondisabled Percent (Standard error)
Audible/visual/tactile info limited	0.60 (0.62)	0.07 (0.07)
Board/exit time inadequate	0	2.21 (1.16)
Boarding/exiting equipment inadequate	0	1.89 (1.50)
Difficult to board/exit	3.38 (1.44)	0.48 (0.37)

(continued)

Table 31
Percent of Disabled and Nondisabled Experiencing Problems on Airplanes During Long-Distance Travel (Continued)

Problems	Disabled Percent (Standard error)	Nondisabled Percent (Standard error)
Equipment storage inadequate	2.76 (1.52)	0.76 (0.58)
Insensitive/unaware crew	1.76 (0.97)	3.40 (1.46)
Insensitive/unaware passengers	3.80 (1.58)	7.06 (2.15)
Left on board without help	0	0
Lighting inadequate	0	0
Obstacles/protusions	0	0.15 (0.15)
Passenger travel info inadequate	0.44 (0.45)	1.02 (0.64)
Passing space/aisle width limited	8.61 (2.66)	9.32 (2.29)
Personal safety concerns	9.73 (3.58)	12.11 (2.92)
Restroom facilities inadequate	3.35 (1.63)	7.07 (2.27)
Seating inadequate	68.61 (6.13)	52.44 (3.73)
Service animals not permitted	0	0.53 (0.54)
Staff assistance/sensitivity poor	4.83 (2.62)	3.31 (1.11)
Wheelchair damaged	0	0
Wheelchair space inadequate	0.53 (0.48)	0
Other airline problem	4.25 (1.72)	12.75 (2.06)
Bad quality of food/no food	12.56 (3.17)	15.48 (2.66)
Long waits/delays before takeoff	3.78 (1.34)	7.47 (1.97)

SOURCE: U.S. Department of Transportation, Bureau of Transportation Statistics, *2002 National Transportation Availability and Use Survey*

TABLES FOR PERSONAL MOTOR VEHICLE OWNERSHIP AND USE

Table 32
Percent of Disabled and Nondisabled by Current Driving Status

Driver status	Disability status	
	Disabled Percent (Standard error)	Nondisabled Percent (Standard error)
Currently driving	**65.28** (1.69)	**88.13** (0.83)

SOURCE: U.S. Department of Transportation, Bureau of Transportation Statistics, *2002 National Transportation Availability and Use Survey*

Table 33
Percent of Disabled and Nondisabled by Number of Days Per Week Drives

	Disability status	
	:---:	:---:
	Disabled	Nondisabled
	Percent	Percent
Number of days per week drives	(Standard error)	(Standard error)
Less than 1 day	3.41 (0.49)	*0.37* *(0.15)*
1	3.88 (0.62)	0.95 (0.25)
2	**9.27** (1.05)	**2.47** (0.41)
3	**10.09** (1.19)	**2.74** (0.43)
4	**7.18** (0.81)	**4.05** (0.46)
5	12.51 (1.58)	9.71 (0.79)
6	**8.80** (1.30)	**12.74** (0.92)
7	**44.85** (2.37)	**66.98** (1.25)
Mean number of days drive per week	**5.12** (0.09)	**6.24** (0.04)

SOURCE: U.S. Department of Transportation, Bureau of Transportation Statistics, *2002 National Transportation Availability and Use Survey*

Table 34
Percent of Disabled and Nondisabled by Number of Vehicles Owned or Leased in Household

	Disability status	
	:---:	:---:
	Disabled	Nondisabled
	Percent	Percent
Number of vehicles owned or leased in household	(Standard error)	(Standard error)
0	**12.58** (0.81)	**4.40** (0.48)
1	**30.21** (1.53)	**21.93** (0.89)
2	**35.68** (1.70)	**39.87** (1.03)
3	**12.77** (1.25)	**18.98** (0.90)
4	**5.10** (0.77)	**7.46** (0.66)
5	**1.54** (0.29)	**4.39** (0.54)
6	*1.68* *(0.56)*	1.74 (0.32)
7	*0.32* *(0.13)*	*0.63* *(0.19)*
8	*0.02* *(0.02)*	*0.20* *(0.12)*
9	*0.07* *(0.05)*	*0.11* *(0.06)*
10	*0.03* *(0.03)*	*0.13* *(0.07)*
More than 10 vehicles	0	*0.17* *(0.13)*

SOURCE: U.S. Department of Transportation, Bureau of Transportation Statistics, *2002 National Transportation Availability and Use Survey*

Table 35

Percent of Disabled and Nondisabled by Number of Vehicles Owned or Leased in Household

	Disability status	
	Disabled	**Nondisabled**
	Percent	**Percent**
Number of vehicles owned or leased in household	**(Standard error)**	**(Standard error)**
0	**12.58**	**4.40**
	(0.81)	(0.48)
1–2	65.89	61.80
	(1.47)	(1.08)
3–4	**17.87**	**26.43**
	(1.36)	(0.99)
5 or more	**3.66**	**7.37**
	(0.66)	(0.64)

SOURCE: U.S. Department of Transportation, Bureau of Transportation Statistics, *2002 National Transportation Availability and Use Survey*

Table 36

Percent of Disabled and Nondisabled Live in a Household that Own or Lease a Vehicle Modified with Adaptive Devices or Equipment for use by Persons with Disabilities

	Disability status	
	Disabled	**Nondisabled**
	Percent	**Percent**
	(Standard error)	**(Standard error)**
Any vehicles modified with adaptive devices or equipment	2.30	*0.31*
	(0.39)	*(0.10)*

SOURCE: U.S. Department of Transportation, Bureau of Transportation Statistics, *2002 National Transportation Availability and Use Survey*

Table 37

Percent of Disabled and Nondisabled that Limit or Restrict Driving

	Disability status	
	Disabled	**Nondisabled**
	Percent	**Percent**
Types of limitations or restrictions	**(Standard error)**	**(Standard error)**
Drive less often than used to	**64.53**	**32.20**
	(2.42)	(1.26)
Avoid driving at night	**51.50**	**25.78**
	(2.21)	(1.08)
Drive less in bad weather	**66.34**	**49.75**
	(2.09)	(1.39)
Avoid high-speed roads and highways	**38.42**	**21.77**
	(1.97)	(1.05)
Avoid busy roads and intersections	**51.67**	**39.98**
	(2.13)	(1.20)
Drive slower than speed limits	**22.02**	**14.92**
	(1.66)	(0.99)
Avoid left hand turns	11.37	8.41
	(1.49)	(0.71)
Avoid driving during rush hours	**57.98**	**41.99**
	(1.90)	(1.44)
Avoid driving unfamiliar roads or places	**38.01**	**27.48**
	(2.08)	(1.05)
Avoid driving distances > 100 miles	**47.24**	**21.91**
	(2.13)	(1.06)

SOURCE: U.S. Department of Transportation, Bureau of Transportation Statistics, *2002 National Transportation Availability and Use Survey*

Table 38
Percent of Disabled and Nondisabled Drivers who Restrict their Driving by Avoiding Driving at Night by Age

Age	Disability status	
	Disabled Percent (Standard error)	Nondisabled Percent (Standard error)
<16	100.00 (0)	46.26 (17.65)
16–24	*24.10* *(8.66)*	21.02 (3.38)
25–34	33.81 (7.70)	20.98 (2.74)
35–44	**44.33** (5.83)	**27.99** (2.87)
45–54	**53.22** (6.22)	**21.23** (2.13)
55–64	**52.95** (4.30)	**30.10** (2.68)
65–74	**56.95** (4.92)	**40.20** (3.12)
75+	**74.38** (3.66)	**54.36** (5.00)

SOURCE: U.S. Department of Transportation, Bureau of Transportation Statistics, *2002 National Transportation Availability and Use Survey*

Table 39
Percent of Disabled and Nondisabled by Driving Ability as Compared to 5 Years Ago

Driving ability	Ability as compared to 5 years ago	Disability status	
		Disabled Percent (Standard error)	Nondisabled Percent (Standard error)
Eyesight/night vision	Worse	**39.62** (1.81)	**28.08** (1.23)
	Same	**55.65** (1.80)	**66.35** (1.36)
	Better	4.74 (0.95)	5.56 (0.63)
Attention span	Worse	**18.51** (1.61)	**4.40** (0.49)
	Same	**72.97** (1.98)	**80.43** (1.26)
	Better	**8.53** (1.18)	**15.18** (1.17)
Hearing	Worse	**20.66** (1.26)	**6.99** (0.57)
	Same	**77.43** (1.29)	**88.18** (0.88)
	Better	**1.91** (0.53)	**4.83** (0.67)
Coordination	Worse	**20.98** (1.52)	**3.58** (0.43)
	Same	**73.58** (1.80)	**85.68** (1.03)
	Better	**5.44** (1.00)	**10.73** (1.00)

(continued)

Table 39
Percent of Disabled and Nondisabled by Driving Ability as Compared to 5 Years Ago (Continued)

| | | Disability status | |
| | | Disabled Percent (Standard error) | Nondisabled Percent (Standard error) |
Driving ability	Ability as compared to 5 years ago		
Reaction time	Worse	**11.73** (1.21)	**3.54** (0.50)
	Same	81.13 (1.45)	77.99 (1.18)
	Better	**7.13** (1.05)	**18.48** (1.17)
Depth perception	Worse	**14.92** (1.64)	**6.98** (0.69)
	Same	80.50 (1.74)	83.22 (1.15)
	Better	**4.57** (1.03)	**9.81** (0.96)

SOURCE: U.S. Department of Transportation, Bureau of Transportation Statistics, *2002 National Transportation Availability and Use Survey*

Table 40
Percent of Disabled and Nondisabled by Reasons to Give up Driving

| | Disability status | |
| | Disabled Percent (Standard error) | Nondisabled Percent (Standard error) |
Reasons to give up driving		
Never plan to give up driving	9.62 (1.18)	11.19 (0.83)
Other transportation was available	*1.28 (0.39)*	3.62 (0.53)
Cannot pass the driver license renewal process	1.54 (0.43)	0.87 (0.24)
Cause crash, accident, injury, or other incident	**5.06** (0.91)	**2.86** (0.44)
Involved in crash, accident, other incident	4.55 (1.16)	2.69 (0.42)
Doctor says to stop driving	4.22 (0.78)	3.67 (0.54)
Family/friend/neighbor convinces to stop driving	2.07 (0.42)	2.41 (0.43)
Police/law enforcement advise stop driving	*1.22 (0.39)*	*0.97 (0.30)*
Feel cannot operate vehicle safely	37.00 (1.79)	33.44 (1.52)
Reach a certain age	**6.40** (1.30)	**10.24** (0.93)
Eyesight declines	33.69 (2.31)	36.93 (1.26)
Hearing declines	5.43 (1.22)	6.04 (0.72)
Other physical limitations	31.34 (2.12)	29.64 (1.22)
Other mental limitations	**5.31** (0.71)	**7.65** (0.72)
Other limitations	11.96 (1.37)	12.55 (0.94)

SOURCE: U.S. Department of Transportation, Bureau of Transportation Statistics, *2002 National Transportation Availability and Use Survey*